W9-DET-117

JUL 2 9 2003

DICTATORSHIP

30036007526963

Richard Tames

Heinemann Library
Chicago, Illinois

Designed by AMR
Originated by Dot Gradations
Printed in Hong Kong by South China Printing

07 06 05 04 03
10 9 8 7 6 5 4 3 2 1

Library of Congress Cataloging-in-Publication Data

Tames, Richard.
   Dictatorship / Richard Tames.
      p. cm. -- (Political and economic systems)
Summary: Discusses the history and theory behind dictatorship as a
political system and explains how it has been applied in practice.
Includes bibliographical references and index.
   ISBN 1-40340-318-X
   1. Dictatorship--Juvenile literature. [1. Dictatorship.] I. Title.
II. Series.
   JC495 .T36 2003
   321.9--dc21
                              2002006315

Acknowledgements
The publishers would like to thank the following for permission to reproduce photographs:
Hulton Archive, pp. 6, 8, 26, 31, 37; Corbis/Bill Gentile, p. 11; Corbis/Charles Lenars, p. 16;
Bridgeman/British Museum, p. 17; Corbis/Bettmann, pp. 20, 28, 32, 40, 42; Kobal Collection, p. 21;
Corbis/Archivo Iconografico, p. 24; Bridgeman, p. 25; Corbis/Christel Gerstenberg, p. 35;
Corbis/Sygma/Lundt Dimitri, p. 44; Rex, p. 45; Corbis/Sygma/Robert Patrick, p. 50; Corbis/David
and Peter Turnley, p. 53.

Cover photograph: Supporters of Saddam Hussein, reproduced with permission of Associated Press.

Every effort has been made to contact copyright holders of any material reproduced in this book.
Any omissions will be rectified in subsequent printings if notice is given to the publishers.

Our thanks to Christopher Gibb for his comments in the preparation of this book.

Disclaimer
All the Internet addresses (URLs) given in this book were valid at the time of going to press. However,
due to the dynamic nature of the Internet, some addresses may have changed, or sites may have ceased
to exist since publication. While the author and publishers regret any inconvenience this may cause
readers, no responsibility for any such changes can be accepted by either the author or the publishers.

Some words are shown in bold, **like this.** You can find out what they
mean by looking in the glossary.

Contents

The Night of the Long Knives

On June 29, 1934, dozens of tough-looking men wearing brown uniform shirts came together from all over Germany to meet at a hotel in the lakeside resort of Bad Wiesee. Respectable Germans disliked these rowdy bullies, but they were also afraid of them. They were members of the **SA—Sturmabteilung** ("Storm Troopers")—the **Nazi** party's **militia.** The Nazi party under Adolf Hitler had been the government of Germany since January 1933. SA men strutted the streets, drilled and practiced with weapons, and looked forward to ever more power in the new Nazi Germany.

The SA's top commander, Ernst Röhm, had launched Hitler's political career. He was confident that Hitler supported his plan to absorb the regular German army into the SA, with himself in command. Röhm could not have been more wrong. Hitler felt that the SA was too big and dangerously out of his direct control. He now wanted to work with the professional armed forces to rearm Germany. He wanted to win the support of respectable Germans by making the country prosperous again.

Hitler arrived unexpectedly early at Bad Wiesee on the morning of June 30, 1934. Röhm and the other top SA leaders were still asleep. They were quickly disarmed, arrested, and taken away by Hitler's personal bodyguards, the black-uniformed **SS:** the **Schutzstaffel** ("defense squadron"). They were taken to the Nazi party headquarters in Munich, where they were shot. There were other executions without trial throughout the country. Not all of those executed were SA men. Others were political opponents who Hitler was able to get rid of as part of the same operation.

It was announced that Röhm had been planning to seize power for himself. It was officially admitted that eighty-seven plotters had been killed. The real number was probably hundreds. Newspapers were forbidden to publish details of the victims and all documents connected with "the measures taken on 30 June, 1 and 2 July" were destroyed, so no one could be sure. On July 4, at a special ceremony, Hitler personally presented each SS executioner with a special dagger to honor their loyalty to him. On July 13, he told the German Reichstag **(parliament),** "If any one . . . asks why I did not turn to the regular courts . . . then all I can say to him is this: in this hour I was responsible for the fate of the German people and thereby I became the supreme judge on behalf of the German people. . . . I gave the orders to shoot the ringleaders in this treason. . . ."

Leaders of the world's **democracies** were as horrified to hear Hitler's claim that he stood above the law as they were at his open use of murder. Among ordinary German people, however, there was widespread approval. They believed the fake evidence of a plot and applauded Hitler's merciless action against the alleged plotters. Germany's generals were pleased to see SA plans to take over the military ended. Germany's leading law professor, Carl Schmitt of Berlin University, praised Hitler's direct justice.

Less than a month later, Germany's aged president, Paul von Hindenburg, died. Hitler then simply merged the vacant position of president with his own post of **chancellor.** He made himself commander-in-chief, with the single title of Führer (leader). All officers, soldiers, and government officials from then on were forced to swear a personal oath of loyalty and obedience to Adolf Hitler, the Führer of the German Reich and German People. By executing men in his own militia, Hitler had shown that even his loyal supporters were not safe from his **arbitrary** power. He had taken one more decisive step toward making himself dictator—sole master—of Europe's biggest nation.

Forms of dictatorship can be traced back to ancient Greece, but Adolf Hitler ranks with Joseph Stalin of the **Soviet Union** and Mao Zedong of China as an example of the new type of dictator made possible by technology in the twentieth century.

Here, Hitler gives a speech at the microphone. He spent many hours rehearsing, not only his speeches, but also the dramatic gestures that went with them.

The styles of government they created are known as **totalitarian** because these men aimed at total control over the people they governed. No aspect of ordinary people's lives—the friends they had, what they read, how they passed their **leisure** time—was considered to be a purely private matter outside politics. Dictators have always had the negative aim of crushing opposition to their rule. In modern times, they have also had the positive aim of transforming the countries they governed.

Sayings of the dictators

Adolf Hitler
"I learned the use of terror from the **communists,** of slogans from the Catholic church, and the use of **propaganda** from the **democracies.**"
"The greater the lie, the greater the chance it will be believed."
"With us the Leader and the Idea are one and every party member has to do what the leader orders."
"In starting and waging a war it is not right that matters, but victory."

Joseph Stalin
"We are fifty or a hundred years behind the advanced countries. We must make good this distance within ten years. Either we do it or they crush us."
"A single death is a tragedy: a million is a statistic."

Mao Zedong
"Political power grows out of the barrel of a gun."
"A revolution is not a dinner party or writing an essay or doing embroidery. A revolution is an act of violence. . . ."

② What Makes a Dictatorship?

Adolf Hitler's ruthless treatment of his own supporters on the Night of the Long Knives shows a number of the key features of a modern dictatorship.

Concentration of power

Decision-making is in the hands either of a single dictator or of a small committee. There are no legal checks and balances against the abuse of power except the failure of the system to act efficiently itself. This can happen when the dictator rewards loyal followers with jobs that they are too corrupt or incompetent to carry out, or when they work against each other to increase their personal power.

Arbitrary rule

The **constitution,** if there is one, is largely meaningless in practice. Laws are either ignored or misapplied. There is no effective **rule of law. Secret police** operate outside of the law to spy on and destroy any opposition. Dictatorships readily and routinely use violence to hold back opposition. They have their opponents imprisoned, murdered, or driven out of the country and into **exile.** However, dictatorships cannot be based on violence and repression alone. At the very least they need the obedience of the police, armed forces, or party **militia** they rely on to use violence against their opponents.

A ruling ideology

An **ideology** is a set of ideas that explains a political program. **Democracies** tolerate differing ideas about both the methods and aims of politics. Dictatorships, on the other hand, force people to accept a single ideology. This ideology is the officially approved view of what politics ought to achieve and which methods should be used to achieve it. Other aims and methods are **suppressed.** The main instrument for imposing an ideology is usually a political party led by the dictator. Normally it is the only permitted party, but it is often supported by other organizations, such as a militia, a youth movement, or a women's group.

Mussolini, in Fascist Party uniform, hails an adoring crowd in Italy. Many dictatorships have been genuinely popular and needed little force to maintain their power. Mussolini's rousing speeches excited and flattered his followers into believing they were building a great new future for Italy.

Core supporters

Winning the active support of at least part of the general population limits the need to use violence and is essential for stability. Depending on the country, crucial groups of supporters might include large landowners, trade unions, tribal chiefs, students, or religious institutions.

In the twentieth century, dictatorships usually wanted much more than mere obedience. They aimed to get the bulk of the population involved in carrying out political programs. These programs might include redistributing land, building up industry, or expanding the armed forces.

Successful dictatorships have recruited supporters to serve as party officials, **militia** officers, and so on. These supporters were rewarded with well-paid jobs and a voice in the system. Dictatorships also gained more passive, less committed support from groups that benefited from their rule. These benefits may be material, such as land, jobs, healthcare, or education. They may also be psychological, like pride in one's country or race, expulsion of a foreign ruler, overthrow of a cruel government, defeat of a hated enemy, or order and stability after a period of chaos.

Throughout the twentieth century, **democracy** and dictatorship were rival systems of government. There have been periods during which it seemed dictatorships would be more successful than democracies. In Europe in the 1920s, for example, **fascism** was on the rise. Then, in the 1950s, **communism** seemed to spread through every continent. In the 1970s, many newly independent countries in Asia and Africa lurched between dictatorship and chaos. In the end, however, these governments did not last. Fascism was smashed by defeat in World War II. Communism in many countries collapsed or was weakened when the **Soviet Union** broke up in 1989–1991. Throughout Asia, Africa, and Latin America many dictatorships have given way to democracies. For the moment at least, democracies seem to have claimed success.

Explaining their politics

Fascism

"Fascism is a religion: the twentieth century will be known as the century of fascism."
"For the fascist, everything is in the state and nothing human or spiritual exists, much less has value, outside the state."
"Fascism believes that permanent peace is neither possible nor useful."
Benito Mussolini

"A creed entirely given over to hate, to irreverence and to violence."
Pope Pius XI

Nazism

"We must develop organizations in which an individual's entire life can take place. Then every activity and every need of every individual will be regulated . . . by the party . . . there are no longer any free realms in which the individual belongs to himself. . . . The time of personal happiness is over." Adolf Hitler

Communism

"The theory of communism may be summed up in one sentence : Abolish all private property." Karl Marx and Friedrich Engels
"Communism has nothing to do with love. It is an excellent hammer which we use to destroy our enemy." Mao Zedong

③ Styles of Dictatorship

Many dictatorships have had the outward trappings of democratic government—a **constitution,** elections, newspapers, even **demonstrations.** In a dictatorship, though, these do not affect how the political system actually works—through corruption, force, fraud, terror, and trickery.

Democracies have a more or less family resemblance to one another. They are based either on some variant form of the American or French presidential **republics** or the British "Westminster model" of **parliamentary** government. Dictatorships, by contrast, developed in many guises, though they often borrowed techniques from one another.

The **fascist regimes** of Italy (1922–1943) and Germany (1933–1945) and their imitators and allies before and during World War II were based on the idea of an inspired man of destiny. This man was supposed to be able to transform his nation by winning the eager, disciplined support of the people.

The *caudillismo* of Latin America and Spain continued the nineteenth-century traditions of the rule of a strongman. *Caudillos* were supported by the armed forces and by the Roman Catholic church in the interests of order and stability. Sometimes they borrowed the outward style of **fascism,** in terms of such things as party uniforms, **propaganda,** youth movements, and mass rallies. They usually aimed to keep things as they were, however, rather than bring about great changes.

In 1973, Argentina's former dictator, Juan Péron, returned from **exile** to be freely elected as president. He died the following year after failing to tackle the country's economic problems. In 1976, the military seized power, banned all political parties, and carried on a "dirty war" against any opponents who dared to challenge its rule. About 15,000 people "disappeared" and must be presumed dead. In 1982, to distract Argentines from their problems, the **junta** leader General Galtieri ordered the invasion of the British-occupied Falkland Islands, which Argentina had long claimed as its own.

FOR MORE INFORMATION ON PÉRON AND PINOCHET, SEE PAGES 59–60.

For a few weeks the military was popular, but when Britain recaptured the islands Galtieri was forced from power. **Civilian** rule was then restored.

Chilean **military dictator** Augusto Pinochet (with sash) reviews a military parade. From the 1960s onward, a new form of dictatorship emerged in Latin America. In this new form, senior officers were supported by well-disciplined and old-established armed forces. They were also aided by **technocrats.** With this support and aid, they seized power to solve an economic crisis or crush extremist movements.

Communist states theoretically aimed to free the ordinary people and offer them a better life in a fairer society. In practice, however, they repressed those ordinary people through the use of **secret police, militias,** and party and state officials. Sometimes dictatorial power in communist states was in the hands of small committees of party officials; sometimes power was exercised by a single individual. Some communist states lasted for half a century or more. Others did not last nearly that long. For example, Colonel Mengistu Haile Mariam's government in Ethiopia (1977–1991) called itself communist. However, because they were constantly at war with opponents or neighboring countries, they failed to establish lasting regimes.

In Africa and Asia, former European **colonies** became independent countries from the 1940s onward. A wide range of **regimes** have existed since that time. The regimes have varied greatly in what they claimed to represent and in the degree of bloodshed and chaos they caused. There have been two main types of dictatorship in these countries.

The first is the **civilian** system. This system is based on a single ruling political party that is headed by a **charismatic** politician. This person is often the leader of a movement for national independence. A good example is Kwame Nkrumah (1909–1972), ruler of Ghana from its independence in 1957 to his overthrow by the army in 1966.

The second type of dictatorship is the military regime. This system is based on newly-established armed forces. It is often headed by a junior or newly promoted and inexperienced officer, such as Idi Amin, dictator of Uganda from 1971 to 1979.

Both types of dictatorship have often been split by conflicts between different tribes, regions, or ethnic or religious groups. Both have tended to become personal systems of rule. These systems have proved incapable either of delivering effective government or of building strong regimes which would outlast the dictator himself. They might genuinely try to turn a political vision into reality, such as transforming a poor agricultural country into a modern industrial one. Many, though, simply became robber regimes. They treated the **state** as the private property of the dictator, to be used for his personal benefit and to buy the loyalty of such people as favored generals and business leaders.

Dictators and monarchs

Although dictatorship was known in the ancient world, it did not become common until the nineteenth century. For most of human history states have been governed by **monarchs.** Unlike modern dictators, monarchs rarely based their claim to rule on their personality or the need to carry out some political program.

Normally a king had to be of royal blood. He was usually the son or brother of the previous ruler. If he was not a family member, he was at least chosen by the ruler. A new ruler was often confirmed in office by a **coronation** or some form of acceptance by a council of powerful nobles or priests. Although some kings did act like modern dictators, ruling by terror or ordering the killing of their opponents, many accepted limits to their power. These limits were usually set by law, custom, or religion. Kings acknowledged that even they were subject to some higher power. Unlike kings, who usually inherit their position, dictators must justify their right to rule by claiming to be extraordinary men or promising to do extraordinary things.

This is a bust of the young Roman emperor Caligula (ruled A.D. 37–41). Occasionally, traditional monarchs behaved as arbitrarily as modern dictators. Rulers whose cruelty seemed totally **arbitrary**, like the Roman emperors Caligula or Commodus (ruled A.D. 180–192) —both of whom came to believe that they actually were gods—usually ended up being murdered, often by their own bodyguards.

13

Machiavelli: principles or power ?

From the fourteenth century onward, Italy came to resemble ancient Greece. It was divided into a number of contending **city-states,** which were frequently at war with one another. Some were ruled by princes. Others were **republics** in form, but were actually ruled by the head of a powerful family who was a prince in everything except the actual name. Florence was run by the fabulously rich Medici family for three centuries. They became celebrated as generous patrons of poets and painters who often glorified them in return.

These princely rulers were known as **despots.** Like modern dictators, they wanted all power to be in their own hands. They were constantly on guard against rivals, whom they were prepared to imprison or even murder. Like modern dictators, they often claimed to be ruling for the benefit of their people. They justified their personal power by saying that it was necessary to guard against foreign enemies. Unlike modern dictators, however, they had no ambition to control the lives of their subjects in detail, providing they were content to stay out of politics. Also unlike modern dictators, they had to at least pretend to respect Christian teachings and the authority of the Church.

Beginning in the Middle Ages, many handbooks were written to tell rulers how they should govern. Almost all were written by churchmen, who naturally declared that rulers should follow the teachings of the Church and be truthful, generous, just, and merciful. *The Prince*, written by Niccolo Machiavelli (1469–1527) in 1513, was quite different and brutally realistic. Machiavelli had worked for the republican government of Florence until it was overthrown in 1512. He lost his job and used his enforced retirement to write about what he had learned. Machiavelli knew from first-hand experience that real Italian politics was full of blackmail, betrayal, and murder. His starting-point was his own rather low opinion of human nature: "One can make this generalization about men: they are ungrateful, fickle, liars and deceivers, they avoid danger and are greedy for profit. . . ."

Machiavelli wrote at a time when Italy had been invaded by both French and Spanish armies and was reduced to a battleground. As an Italian who wanted to see the foreigners driven out and order restored, Machiavelli hoped that a strong and ruthless leader would emerge to do the job. The main purpose of *The Prince* was to show such a man how to gain power and, having gained power, how to use it and keep it. The most important quality a ruler needed was what Machiavelli called *virtu*. This word can be translated as "guts" or "nerve"—the willingness to do what needs to be done in an uncertain world of unseen threats, sudden dangers, and unpredictable crises.

Machiavelli warned rulers against being cruel for pleasure and advised them to make their subjects prosperous and contented. He knew that anyone with power has enemies as a matter of course. It would be foolish to add to the number of enemies without good cause. When it was essential to act, though, there should be no holding back. "The injury done to a man ought to be such that you do not need to fear his revenge."

Models for Machiavelli

Some scholars believe that Machiavelli had the career of Cosimo de Medici (1389–1464) in mind when he was writing about a perfect prince. Cosimo used a fortune made from banking to bribe his way to power in Florence. He kept up the pretense that it was a republic. However, he filled all positions of power with his trusted supporters who constantly renewed his right to rule as a dictator. In theory his powers were purely temporary, but in practice they were permanent. Cosimo also used his money to hire troops from the Sforza family of Milan. In doing so, he freed himself from the need to keep the Florentines personally loyal. Cosimo ruled Florence from 1434 until his death. The Medicis ruled Florence almost continuously until 1737.

Machiavelli also certainly knew and admired Cesare Borgia (1475–1507), the illegitimate son of Pope Alexander VI, who made him an archbishop when he was only seventeen. A brilliant lawyer, Cesare proved to be an equally outstanding commander of the Pope's army, conquering large parts of central Italy. He had his own brother-in-law murdered and executed army commanders who plotted against him. He still lost his power when his father—who was probably poisoned—died.

Machiavelli knew that rulers are faced with life and death decisions that ordinary citizens do not face. Therefore, to stay in power, they had to do things which would be wrong for a private individual. "Politics," he wrote, "have no relation to morals." Machiavelli also realized that appearance and reality are two different things and a prince should try at least to look like a good man: "He should appear to be merciful, faithful to his word, kind, straightforward, and religious. . . . But his character should be such that if he needs to be the opposite he knows how. . . . [A] prince, and especially a new prince, cannot observe all those things which give men a reputation for virtue, because in order to defend his **state** he is often forced to act against good faith, kindness, charity, or religion . . . so he should be flexible . . ., he should not depart from what is good, if that is possible, but he should know how to do evil, if that is necessary."

Machiavelli's frankness made his name a byword for wickedness. Deceit, betrayal, plotting, and assassination came to be denounced as "Machiavellian." Some thinkers, however, believed that Machiavelli should be praised for writing about politics as it really was, not as it ought to be.

The possibilities of power

The power of traditional monarchies to harm or even interfere with the lives of their ordinary subjects depended on the resources and technologies they could use. Only the richest rulers had permanent armies. Most had to rely on forces supplied by powerful nobles or of subject peoples, either of whom might revolt if treated too badly. Travel was usually difficult and often dangerous. Warfare was largely seasonal, rarely happening in winter. Politics concerned only a tiny elite. The mass of the population was unquestioningly loyal to the king unless actually driven to revolt. Nobody liked paying the taxes which the king used to pay his soldiers, judges, and officials. Nevertheless, most people valued a strong **monarchy** that defended them from invaders and punished banditry.

Traditional monarchies were supported by religious **ideologies.** Christianity, Islam, and Buddhism all taught that the world was ordered by a divine power. This divine power was represented on earth by rulers who governed righteously as long as they upheld religion's teachings. Obedience to religion would be rewarded in the afterlife.

What modern dictatorships can set out to do and the ways they can rule are far less limited than the opportunities allowed to traditional monarchs. **Industrialization** has greatly increased the wealth governments can use to create mass **literacy** and employ vast numbers of officials, armed forces, and police. The clock-based timetable, the typewriter, and the telephone made it possible to regulate and control in detail the lives of the mass of citizens.

A powerful limit on rulers' ambitions has been weakened by the decline in religious belief. If people no longer believe in the supreme importance of life after death, they may be more eager to follow a leader who promises them power and prosperity in their life on earth. Modern ideologies, such as **communism** and **fascism,** look toward the future but claim to transform life now for the better.

This coin bears the head of Elizabeth I, looking suitably grand and dignified. Until very recently, most people never saw their ruler, except, perhaps as a face on a coin.

Allah's will

In the Islamic world some governments base their right to rule on the claim that they are enforcing Allah's laws.

In 1979, the shah (king) of Iran was overthrown by a mass movement led by the country's religious leaders. The Islamic **republic** that was created has an elected **parliament.** Parliament's laws and decisions, however, are subject to review by the chief Ayatollah ("Sign from Allah"), an expert in Islamic law. The Ayatollah then rules whether or not the new laws conform to Allah's wishes.

Saudi Arabia is a **monarchy,** but claims to have no **constitution** except the Qur'an, the holy scripture of Islam. It also has no parliament, political parties, or voters. The king, guided by Islam, rules by **decree.**

Afghanistan was ruled from 1994 to 2001 by the extremist Taliban ("Seeker") movement. The Taliban enforced a cruel code of conduct on ordinary people, based on a crude version of Islam which ignored the interpretations and teachings of the religion's learned scholars. Women were entirely forbidden to go to school or work. Men were beaten if they did not grow long beards. Television, music, and sports were banned. Rather than being based on religion, the Taliban government was simply based on force. The Taliban's rules were rejected by the Afghan people as soon as its power to use violence was broken.

Communist dictatorships set out to destroy the power of organized religion. They closed churches, seized church property, imprisoned priests, and used the school system to attack religious beliefs. The **Nazis** treated Christianity as though it were out of date and irrelevant. They even tried to develop a **pagan** alternative, based on ancient German gods and legends. In fascist Italy, where the Roman Catholic church was too powerful to ignore, Mussolini used its fear of communism to limit its criticisms of his rule. On the whole, the church accepted **fascism** as better than chaos or communism.

New technologies

New technologies have given dictators the power to use violence on a whole new scale. In the past, mobs of rebellious peasants armed with farmyard tools often defeated regular soldiers, at least for a while. Today, these mobs would be easily **massacred** by professional troops with armored vehicles and rapid-firing weapons. Ivan the Terrible ruled Russia brutally from 1547 to 1584 and was responsible for killing thousands who rebelled against his rule. However, he was only able to enforce his power through men riding on horses, armed with swords and primitive guns.

This is a portrait of Ivan the Terrible. Comparatively few of his subjects would have known what he looked like during his reign. This impression of him was painted by the Russian artist Viktor Vasnetsov nearly 350 years after his reign.

Joseph Stalin was dictator of the **Soviet Union** from 1928 to 1953. He killed millions of peasants who opposed his land reforms. Using police forces and **militias** with machine-guns and artillery, he ordered mass murders. He also created famines by controlling trucks, tanks, and railways and cutting off food supplies to whole regions.

New technologies of communication have brought the rulers and the ruled much closer. Cheap printing, photography, radio, and film allow rulers to communicate directly with their people. The subjects of Ivan the Terrible might never have seen him in person or in print. The citizens of Soviet Russia, though, saw Stalin's face everywhere—in newspapers and magazines, on posters, and in school textbooks. Every town had a statue of him. Every year tens of thousands of people marched in great parades in front of him; tens of millions could witness these events through radio and newsreels.

Stalin's purges

Lenin's death in 1924 was followed by a power struggle from which Stalin emerged as victor by 1928. He then introduced a series of Five-Year Plans intended to transform the U.S.S.R. into a modern industrial nation and bring all farming under state control. By taking land from the richer peasants (*kulaks*) and confiscating grain from the rest, Stalin caused a famine that killed over six million people.

In 1934, Stalin ordered the murder of Sergei Kirov, a local communist leader in Leningrad whose popularity he saw as a threat to his own position. Kirov's death was then used as a pretext for the arrest and trial of hundreds and then thousands of loyal communists on made-up charges of terrorism, plotting, or sabotaging industry. The "purge" of suspected traitors was then extended to the armed forces, leading to the execution or imprisonment of 35,000 officers. By 1938, about eight million people had been arrested and just under seven million people had been sent to labor camps where they were forced to work building roads, dams, factories, and power supplies. Less than 3 percent survived the standard ten-year sentence. When Stalin died in 1953, twelve million prisoners were still in labor camps.

A nightmare vision

The English **socialist** George Orwell (1903–1950) wrote his novel *Nineteen Eighty-four* immediately after World War II. The full horrors of **Nazism** were being revealed and the communist U.S.S.R., under Stalin, was taking over the former **democracies** of eastern Europe.

In *Nineteen Eighty-four*, the world is divided into three empires, constantly at war with each other. The war is actually not real; the Party, symbolized by Big Brother, tells people there is a war to justify the Party's complete power, claiming ever-present dangers from traitors and enemies. These dangers require the constant use of torture and terror. Every home is fitted with "telescreens" so the government can spy on everyone all the time. There is no privacy. Children are rewarded for telling the Thought Police if their parents say anything against the Party or Big Brother. There is no such thing as private life and citizens have no rights at all. Everyone must dedicate their life to the Party and support it totally.

The hero of *Nineteen Eighty-four*, Winston Smith, is a victim of the system that oppresses him and everyone else outside the leadership of the Party. He is employed at the Ministry of Truth, constantly rewriting history so that no one can challenge the Party's complete control of information. This control is strengthened by the spread of Newspeak, a deliberately simplified form of English designed to end free thought by destroying the power to make contrasts or distinctions. In Newspeak, the words "wrong," "immoral," "wicked," and "evil" are replaced by the all-purpose term "doubleplusungood."

Winston challenges the whole system and pays the price. He is tortured until he agrees that two plus two makes five, and truly believes that they do so. He is tortured until he not only obeys the Party, but sincerely loves the idea of Big Brother.

This is a still from a film version of *Nineteen Eighty-four* made in 1984. The book was written as a warning, rather than a prophecy—a picture of what could happen, not what inevitably would happen.

The Origins of Dictatorship

Dictatorship is essentially a modern type of government, but it has had forerunners in the past that have inspired some of its forms and features. Modern dictators have sometimes been inspired by the examples set by great historical figures of the ancient world, such as Julius Caesar, or by military adventurers, such as Oliver Cromwell and Napoleon Bonaparte.

Ancient Greece

Greek thinkers recognized an oppressive form of one-man rule. They called it **tyranny.** The tyrant either ignored the law and seized power by force of arms, or inherited his position from someone who had. Because tyranny usually rested on the personal qualities of the tyrant—ambition, toughness, military skill, courage, and ruthlessness—tyrannical rule often ended with the death of the tyrant or the overthrow of a successor too weak to hang on to power. Tyranny therefore was thought of as a form of rule that was basically unstable.

Tyrants were also installed by foreign powers, such as Persia and Macedonia, to rule conquered Greek **city-states** on their behalf. These tyrannies could last longer because the power of the tyrant depended less on personal qualities than on the use of foreign troops to hold back opposition.

Greek thinkers saw that in some situations tyranny might have value—bringing order after war, for example, or helping to make a change-from rule by a small **aristocracy** to a more **democratic** form of government. Individual tyrants were sometimes great builders or generous patrons of artists and poets. More often, though, tyrants abused their power and acted cruelly, and the Greeks came to disapprove of tyranny.

Rome

Dictatorship in the early Roman **republic** was almost the opposite of what it became in the twentieth century. It arose from emergency situations, such as the need to suppress a rebellion, but it was a legal position, intended to last only for a limited time.

The dictator was given complete power by the senate, Rome's supreme law-making body, but only for a maximum of six months. Any abuse of power might be punished afterward by the law.

The ambitious Roman general Sulla (138 to 78 B.C.E.) was appointed dictator in 82 B.C.E. after a civil war. He used his power to have dozens of political opponents murdered. By packing the senate with his supporters, he got it to declare his actions legal. His deeds later inspired another ambitious general, Julius Caesar (c.102 to 44 B.C.E.). He was also appointed dictator after a civil war and then dictator for life. When he had his head put on coins, like a king, members of the old aristocracy who controlled the senate saw that Caesar was turning his position into a **monarchy.** They murdered him to preserve the republic. His murder started another, even worse, civil war which destroyed republican government completely.

France—crises in contrast

In the early stages of the French Revolution, when a republic had just been established, it was threatened by anti-revolutionary armies of **exiles** along its borders. Thousands of prisoners, accused of being enemies of the revolution in France, were **massacred** without trial. The revolutionary government came under the control of a fanatical lawyer, Maximilien Robespierre (1758–1794). Like a Roman dictator defending the state in an hour of crisis, he continued the Reign of Terror until French victories ended the crisis.

In 1958, the French Fourth Republic collapsed over the future of Algeria, a French **colony** fighting for its independence. Party leaders appealed to retired war hero General Charles de Gaulle (1890–1970). He had liberated France from **Nazi** occupation, restored **democracy,** and served briefly as the first post-war head of government. As a man above politics, he was asked to take power and rescue France from the risk of a military coup or even civil war. De Gaulle used his position to draw up a **constitution** for a new Fifth Republic with greatly strengthened powers for the president, a position de Gaulle himself held until 1969. He thus played the role of a Roman-style dictator, using temporary powers to reestablish constitutional government, rather than to end it.

This portrait of Robespierre shows him as a calm, well-groomed lawyer, but he was thought to be a wild fanatic. He was accused of aiming for a personal dictatorship and guillotined without trial.

Soldiers of fortune

In medieval Europe successful kings were warriors who usually commanded the army in person. Most nobles were trained as fighting men and peasants were expected to defend their homes. During the sixteenth century, full-time professional armies came into being. With these full-time armies came the possibility that an ambitious general could use his army to seize power for himself.

Oliver Cromwell (1599–1658)

The abolition of the British **monarchy** in 1649 after the civil war and the execution of Charles I was followed by political confusion. Oliver Cromwell became a **military dictator.** Although he tried different systems, he could find no other way to govern. Even though he refused the crown, he lived in a palace, had his image put on coins, and took the title "Lord Protector of the Commonwealth." Cromwell's conquests brought the entire British Isles under one ruler for the first time, but he failed to provide for a successor. On his deathbed Cromwell chose his son Richard to succeed him, but Tumbledown Dick (as he was nicknamed) had been kept out of politics and was simply ignored. Another former general, George Monck (1608–1670), arranged to restore the monarchy and was royally rewarded for it. Cromwell remained a unique figure in British history, inspiring no further imitators as military dictator in Britain.

This portrait shows Cromwell as a royal figure, much like the king he had executed. Cromwell was an obscure, unambitious English country gentleman. Civil war (1642–1649) revealed his unexpected talent as a commander of the victorious Parliamentary army.

Napoleon Bonaparte (1769–1821)

Unlike Cromwell, Napoleon had been a professional soldier since his youth. He was also intensely ambitious. His military brilliance and the extraordinary opportunities created by the French Revolution made him an army commander at the young age of 26. Napoleon soon turned military glory into political power. First he became a member of the government, then leader of the government for life. Finally, he crowned himself emperor (1804).

As emperor Napoleon gave France the code of laws still in force today and conquered most of Europe before being defeated. He died in **exile,** a prisoner of the British.

Napoleon's extraordinary career inspired his nephew, Louis-Napoleon (1808–1873), known as Napoleon III, to a life of conspiracy and exile until he, too, managed to come to power under a French **republic.** He imitated his uncle by overthrowing the republic to put himself on the throne of a Second Empire (1852–1870). His reign, too, was smashed by military defeat, this time by Prussia in 1870. Napoleon III died in exile in Britain.

Caudillismo
Simon Bolivar (1783–1830) was dictator successively of Venezuela, Colombia, and Peru. He aimed to give each of these former Spanish colonies a republican government. He also hoped to bring all of the Spanish-speaking **states** of the region into a single unit, similar to the United States. This dream failed. Bolivia, formerly Upper Peru, became a separate state, named in his honor.

An idealized portrait of Simon Bolivar shows him as a fearless and inspiring front-line commander. Noble by birth and a lawyer by training, Bolivar led the armies that freed the colonies of South America from Spanish rule.

Bolivar's career inspired many imitators, most of them with far less noble motives. In the 1820s, the newly independent countries of Latin America were in much the same position that **post-colonial** states in Africa found themselves in the 1960s—rich in resources, but poor in educated manpower. National unity was held back by poor communications and ethnic divisions.

Many countries fell under the rule of *caudillos*. Some of these rulers controlled a whole country, others only a region. (In Latin America a region might be as big as a small country such as Belgium or Denmark.) In many cases the *caudillos* relied on private armies to enforce their will. Armies members were recruited from the peasants who worked the *caudillos'* vast estates. Juan Manuel de Rosas (1793–1877) raised a private army to seize power in Argentina. He ruled by terror until his overthrow in 1852. He then escaped to exile in England. In Paraguay, Francisco Solano López (1827–1870) modeled himself on Napoleon and provoked a catastrophic five-year war against Brazil, Uruguay, and Argentina. It took Paraguay two generations to recover from it.

Full-scale wars between states were relatively rare in Latin America. Thus, in many countries the underemployed militaries were tempted to interfere in politics. This pattern of change of government by *golpe* (coup) and rule by a *junta* (council) of military commanders occurred repeatedly. Since winning independence from Spain in 1825, Bolivia has had over sixty revolutions and eleven **constitutions.** Chile and Uruguay were unusual in developing stable republics (for a time) controlled by **civilian** politicians, changing power through peaceful elections.

Offspring of war

In terms of world politics, nineteenth-century Latin America was a blind alley. It was largely isolated from the rest of world and mostly free from foreign interference.

Because of modern communications in the twentieth century, however, the politics of different **states** and regions affect one another much more. Countries trade with partners on opposite sides of the world. Large armed forces can operate thousands of miles from their homes because they can be transported and supplied almost anywhere. Information travels almost instantaneously. The result has been a growing instability that has often destroyed political systems, opening the way to dictatorships.

In Europe, the **communist** U.S.S.R., **fascist** Italy, and **Nazi** Germany emerged after World War I (1914–1918) had destroyed the empires of Russia, Germany, and Austria-Hungary. Fascist Italy and Nazi Germany in turn helped create General Franco's **regime** in Spain (1939–1975) and various puppets and imitators in World War II.

Mao Zedong proclaims the establishment of the People's Republic of China in 1949. China then helped communists come to power in North Korea and North Vietnam.

FOR DETAILS ON MAO AND OTHER DICTATORS, SEE PAGES 59–60.

A world apart

Albania's mountainous landscape hinders communications. The unique location enabled its people to defeat invasion by Fascist Italy. It also helped Enver Hoxha to cut them off from the outside world.

Hoxha rose to power in the Albanian National Liberation Movement, formed with the aid of Tito's Yugoslav partisans. Declaring Albania a People's Republic in 1946, Hoxha made himself prime minister, foreign minister, defense minister, and head of the communist party. His government took control of all farming and industry. It also banned both Christianity and Islam to make Albania the world's only officially atheist state.

Taking aid from the U.S.S.R. and then China, Hoxha eventually quarreled with both for not being communist enough, leaving Albania isolated even among other communist countries. In 1973, 1974, 1975, and 1982 Hoxha had alleged enemies within the government and Albanian Communist Party removed from power and imprisoned or shot. Albania meanwhile became Europe's poorest country.

Communist control broke down after Hoxha's death in 1985, leading to widespread crime, food shortages, and mass unemployment. This bad situation worsened with an influx of ethnic Albanian refugees from neighboring Kosovo. Thousands of Albanians have since fled abroad in search of a better life, while unstable governments at home struggle to undo the damage of half a century's isolation.

World War II enabled the U.S.S.R. to install communist dictatorships throughout eastern Europe. Enver Hoxha (1908–1985) of Albania and Marshal Josip Tito (1892–1980) of Yugoslavia used their anti-fascist **partisan** armies to set up communist dictatorships after the war.

By weakening the overseas empires of Britain, France, and the Netherlands, World War II hastened the independence of their colonies. The new states were often weak and could not control corruption or ethnic, religious, or tribal conflicts. Neither could they cope with economies based on a few crops or raw materials whose value could rise and fall unpredictably. Corruption, conflict, and a chaotic economy create conditions in which the military are likely to intervene, promising order. A **charismatic** leader could also gather support by promising a better future.

How dictatorships are justified

No dictatorship—personal or collective—openly admits to holding power for the benefit of the rulers rather than the ruled. Instead, a dictatorship claims that it will make life better for all. The people quickly discover that their welfare is not what the dictator is most focused on. Most of these dictatorships eventually fall.

Many dictatorships come into being by claiming to replace an existing government that is weak or corrupt. In 1977, General Zia ul-Haq claimed the **civilian** government of Zulfikar Ali Bhutto in Pakistan was corrupt. He created a dictatorship and ruled until he died in an airplane crash in 1988.

The military in Burma (Myanmar) staged a takeover in 1962, claiming that the government had broken the **constitution.** In 1990, a civilian, democratic party won a two-thirds majority in an election. The military refused to recognize it, however.

The incompetence or oppression of a leader is another common excuse for a dictatorship to claim power. For example, in 1966, Ahmed Sukarno, Indonesia's independence leader, was overthrown by General Suharto. Suharto's hugely corrupt **regime,** however, was even worse. He and his supporters wasted Indonesia's natural riches on a massive scale. Popular unrest forced him to resign in 1998.

In some cases, a revolution of the people is successful and a dictator comes forward to defend it. In Mexico, the Institutional Revolutionary Party (PRI) made sure it had a permanent place as leader from the 1920s until 1997.

Perhaps a country is in a state of chaos from repeated revolution attempts, riots, and strikes. In Spain in 1923, General Primo de Rivera took control with the claim that he would restore order. He eventually lost the support of the army and fell from power in 1930. When that happened, further disorder followed and then civil war from 1936 to 1939.

Sometimes, the reasons for a dictatorship are economic, not political. In the 1950s, Colonel Juan Péron made himself ruler of Agentina in order to end foreign influence over the economy. Péron was driven into **exile.** He returned for a second, unsuccessful term of office as elected president in 1973–1974.

The most widely used justification of all is the promise of a better tomorrow. In return for discipline, effort, and sacrifice now, the dictator may say that every citizen can have a better life. Many regimes, such as Iraq under Saddam Hussein (1937–), have used this justification. They claim to be building a society of welfare for all.

⑤ Fascism and Its Friends

Mussolini's Italy

Italy was on the winning side in World War I, but it gained little in return for huge losses and expense. Thousands of ex-soldiers felt betrayed and resentful. A newly-founded **communist** party called for revolution. Benito Mussolini (1883–1945), a war veteran and journalist, recruited *Fasci di Combattimenti* (bands of fighters) to fight the communists. Mussolini claimed to know how history was unfolding. He promised that under his guidance Italy would move forward to a glorious future.

The Italian fascist youth movement, wearing the party's black-shirt uniform, marches. Students, the unemployed, and many ex-servicemen found that the fascist movement offered them comradeship and a sense of purpose that **civilian** life lacked.

The years after World War I saw violent **demonstrations,** organized street-fighting between **fascists** and communists, and the disruption of daily life by repeated strikes. The fear of revolution created a situation in which many longed for the restoration of order, even at the cost of normal political freedoms.

Mussolini claimed to have seized power as a result of a march on Rome in 1922. This myth suited his image as a strongman. In fact, he became prime minister of Italy legally, at the invitation of King Victor Emmanuel III. Over several years, Mussolini's dictatorship came into being. Gradually the fascist party gained full power over politics and the media. It replaced **parliament** with a Chamber of Corporations that was supposed to represent groups such as workers, farmers, and intellectuals. By doing so, it was to have overcome traditional conflicts between employers and workers in the interest of the nation as a whole. Fascist posters proclaimed *Mussolini ha sempre ragione* (Mussolini is always right). They showed images of Il Duce (the leader) as a twentieth-century Caesar who would restore the ancient glories of the Roman empire. Mussolini's power was limited by the strength of the Catholic church, which he was careful not to attack. Mussolini also sidelined the Italian **monarchy** rather than abolishing it. Once he had achieved power, Mussolini used little violence to maintain his position. Four thousand anti-fascists were imprisoned and thousands more beaten up, but only ten were actually killed.

Mussolini poses for a bust of himself as a grim-faced hero.

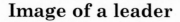

Image of a leader

Both Mussolini and Hitler styled themselves as "Leader" and made sure that the media projected the kind of images they wanted. The kind of image that each chose was very different.

Hitler was usually portrayed as serious, aloof, and distant, almost like a saint, staring into a future that only he had the wisdom to foresee. Mussolini, by contrast, played a variety of roles. Sometimes he was a warrior, decked out in military uniform, sometimes a man of culture, playing the violin, and sometimes a family man, surrounded by his children. He was even photographed, stripped to the waist, helping peasants gather the harvest. For Hitler this kind of image would have been unacceptable. The Italian press was told that Mussolini's name was always to be printed in capital letters and they were never to print pictures that might contradict the image of him as a strongman. For example, they were not allowed to show him dancing or talking to a priest.

Stalin, who ordered or organized the deaths of millions, was frequently portrayed as a kindly father figure, surrounded by crowds of adoring small children, offering him bouquets of flowers. During the war his image incorporated traditional Russian **patriotism**, such as the shadows of past heroes in the background.

Mussolini's attempts to modernize Italy's economy did strengthen industries with military importance, such as the metal and chemical industries. Roads and railways were improved for the same reason. Electricity output tripled between 1920 and 1935. Strikes were banned, along with beauty contests and reports of crime. Population growth was encouraged so that Italy could have a bigger army. As a result, bachelors were taxed for being single, women were banned from government jobs, and everyone employed by the government, from teachers to postmen, was ordered to get married or be fired.

To re-establish Italy as a great power, Mussolini devoted 25 percent of all government spending to the armed forces. His army conquered Ethiopia. He also sent 50,000 troops to fight for Franco in the Spanish Civil War. These adventures were a terrible waste of resources. When Mussolini disastrously decided to join in World War II, Italy simply could not arm its soldiers well enough. Its forces found themselves fighting with tanks, planes, and ships that were far inferior to those of their opponents. Disastrous defeats in the Balkans and North Africa led to an anti-war group among the military. This group overthrew Mussolini in 1943.

The **monarchy,** which still survived, provided an alternative focus for national loyalty. Italian **partisans** fought on the Allied side in World War II against a German army that killed 36,000 of them and shot 10,000 more in **reprisals.** Meanwhile, Mussolini was rescued from imprisonment by **Nazi** special forces. With Nazi backing, he set up a powerless puppet-state, the Republic of Salo. When the Nazis were defeated, Mussolini fled in disguise. He was caught by communist partisans and shot. The war cost Italy a third of its national wealth and left 300,000 dead.

Nazi Germany

In 1933, Hitler, too, came to power by legal means, at the invitation of the president of Germany's **republican** government. He was leader of the largest single party in the Reichstag (German **parliament).** He was supported by experienced political and business leaders who aimed to control him for their own ends. Hitler aimed to crush **communism** and put a powerful Germany at the head of a reorganized Europe. His Germany would be free of Jews, **Slavs,** and other *Untermenschen* (sub-humans), who would be reduced to slavery and eventually wiped out.

Within a month of Hitler's coming to power, the Reichstag burned down. Just how and why was not clear, but it gave Hitler a golden chance to declare a state of emergency and get the members of the Reichstag to grant him the power to rule by **decree.**

The Reichstag itself was soon abolished. Members of the Nazi secret service and armed **militias** were given police powers. A campaign of *Gleichschaltung* (streamlining) removed everyone the Nazis regarded as enemies—Jews, communists, **socialists,** and many leaders of trade unions and churches—from the armed forces, law courts, civil service, education system, big business, and media. Hundreds of thousands of writers, teachers, lawyers, scientists, and artists fled abroad. Hundreds of thousands more were arrested and sent to concentration camps, along with gypsies, homosexuals, and beggars. The Nazis claimed these people would be re-educated through work and lectures. In reality, they were starved, beaten, tortured, or executed.

A **Nazi** election poster claims that a vote for Hitler will free Germany from the chains of despair and humiliation. Hitler's appeal to the German electorate was his promise to restore the nation's shattered pride and put unemployed millions back to work, which he did with speedy success.

35

The **Nazi** takeover of Germany was far more rapid and far more complete than the fascist takeover in Italy. It was also far more bloody. There was no **monarchy** as an alternative focus of loyalty. Divided between Protestant and Catholic, the German churches were also much weaker in their opposition. As Germany was much richer and more technologically advanced than Italy, Nazi dictatorship was much more efficient. Mass-produced radios were installed in every school, railway station, and public building so Hitler could address the entire nation whenever he wanted.

Hitler, unlike Mussolini, did equip his armed forces well. He put Germans back to work, built impressive apartment blocks and *Autobahnen* (expressways), and hosted the 1936 Olympics in Berlin to show off the superiority of the Germans as the world's "Master Race." Unemployment fell from 6 million in 1933 to 300,000 by 1939. Nazi supporters were rewarded with homes, businesses, art treasures, and belongings stolen from Jews. Workers lost the right to free trade unions. In return, they got cheap vacations.

Hitler's aims were summed up in a series of simple slogans. The overriding idea was that the Germans were the world's greatest people. Purged of foreign influences and united by a disciplined movement, the nation would march forward to dominate the world. The idea that Germans should be *"Ein Reich, Ein Volk, Ein Führer"* (one **state,** one people, one leader) led Hitler to demand that Germany's borders should expand to take in all *Auslandsdeutsche*—Germans living under foreign rule. The Nazis did expand Germany's borders. They took control of Austria, the border areas of Czechoslovakia, and the port of Memel in Lithuania. Applying the same aim to Poland is what started World War II in September of 1939.

Crowds and power

Mass-meetings and rallies have been an important feature of dictatorial **regimes.** They provide a substitute for reasoned argument and an opportunity to play on emotions. Both Hitler and Mussolini were brilliant public speakers, able to whip huge crowds into a frenzy of hatred or adoration. Major rallies were carefully stage-managed and often held at night. Flaming torches or blazing searchlights created a dramatic effect in order to concentrate all attention on the leader and drown distractions in the darkness. Every September, Nazis from all over Germany gathered at Nuremberg for a huge rally. In 1936 Hitler told them, "Not every one of you sees me and I do not see every one of you. But I feel you and you feel me . . . we are with him and he with us, and we are now Germany!"

Hitler explained the power of the mass meeting in his book, *Mein Kampf* (*My Struggle*): "in it the individual, who at first . . . feels lonely . . . gets the picture of a larger community which in most people has a strengthening, encouraging effect. . . . [T]he visible . . . agreement of thousands confirms to him the rightness of his new belief. . . . The will, the longing and also the power of thousands are concentrated in every individual."

Hitler arrives at the Berlin Olympic Stadium to address a crowd of 132,000 members of the Hitler Youth organization.

Poland was defeated within weeks. The following spring German armies defeated and occupied Belgium, the Netherlands, Denmark, Norway, and France. That summer they smashed hundreds of miles into the **Soviet Union.** Disastrous German defeats began in 1942, but it took another three years to destroy the **Nazi regime.** Whereas few Italians were prepared to die for **fascism** and many were glad to fight against it, the hold of the Nazi dictatorship over the German people proved much harder to break. The defeat of Nazism cost Germany three-and-a-half million dead, twelve million refugees, and the division of the country into two separate **states** for half a century. Both Fascist Italy and Nazi Germany promised prosperity, but by aggression in war brought defeat which destroyed their achievements.

Imitators and allies

The inter-war regimes of Hungary under Admiral Horthy (1868–1957), Poland under General Pilsudski (1867–1935), Austria under Chancellor Dollfuss (1892–1934), and Portugal under Antonio Salazar (1889–1970) are better described as **authoritarian** than completely dictatorial. All were fiercely anti-communist, but they permitted a limited degree of political freedom for some parties and newspapers. They also respected the influence of the Roman Catholic church. General Franco (1892–1975), commander of the military rebels who had destroyed the Spanish republic in a terrible civil war (1936–1939), refused to be drawn into World War II. Free from outside interference, he made good his hold on power. He ruled until his death in 1975. Before his death, he arranged for the **monarchy** to be restored under King Juan Carlos I, who swiftly returned Spain to **democracy.**

During World War II, the Nazis installed fascist figureheads in short-lived puppet-states they created in Slovakia and Croatia. In Romania General Antonescu (1882–1946) drove King Carol into **exile,** proclaimed himself the nation's *Conducator* (guide), and plunged it into a catastrophic alliance with Germany against the U.S.S.R.

6 What Dictatorships Achieve

The impact of dictatorship varies greatly according to the personality and aims of the dictator and the circumstances he faces. The following examples show a range of possibilities. The first group of dictators can perhaps claim to have had good intentions for their people; the second were simply out to help themselves. These examples also show that there is no simple link between a ruler's intentions and their results, or between a country's natural wealth and its people's prosperity.

Re-making nations

This first group of dictators set out with the aim of remodeling and modernizing their countries to bring greater prosperity to their people.

Atatürk

What is now the **republic** of Turkey was once the core of the sprawling, multi-ethnic **Ottoman empire.** Over six centuries it had spread from its homeland on the Anatolian plateau northward into the Balkans and southward into Arabia. Ruled by a sultan who claimed to be the heir (khalifa, or caliph) of the prophet Muhammad, the empire was based on Islam, but tolerated Christians and Jews.

In the nineteenth century, sultans tried to update their armed forces using mainly German advisers, and the sultan sided with Germany in World War I. Defeat cost the Ottomans most of their territory outside Anatolia and tempted Greece to take more by war. The Greeks were soundly beaten by the Turkish general Mustafa Kemal. Hailed as a hero, Kemal accepted the loss of non-Turkish territories, abolished the Caliphate, and made Turkey a republic with himself as president.

Blaming their defeat in World War I on the backwardness, corruption, and incompetence of Ottoman rule, Kemal aimed to remodel the new Turkey along modern, western lines. His plan not only meant boosting industry, education, and transportation, but changing traditional customs to fit in with

European standards, such as abandoning Arabic script. Kemal threw himself completely into his mission, leading by example under the slogan "Be proud you are Turkish."

Because Turks revered Kemal as a complete **patriot,** head and shoulders above all other leaders, they accepted such dramatic changes as allowing women to vote and moving the capital to Ankara in the heart of Anatolia. All Turks were required to take western-style family names and Kemal became known as Atatürk—Father of the Turks. Islam was too powerful for Atatürk to abolish, but he aimed to keep it out of politics by banning many Islamic organizations and making education purely **secular.** Atatürk's long-term intention was to turn Turkey into a genuine **democracy** with competing political parties, but in his own lifetime he tolerated little opposition to his reforms.

Mustapha Kemal Atatürk (1881–1938), at left, was like a dictator in the Roman sense, rescuing his country from crisis. He set an example of wearing western dress to show Turks what it meant to be a "modern" people.

The depth of national mourning at his death showed that Atatürk was genuinely respected for his achievements. His picture still hangs in every school, post office, town hall, and public building in Turkey. Islam, however, has re-emerged as a force in Turkish politics and the Turkish armed forces have intervened in politics periodically as the self-appointed guardians of Kemalism.

The Pahlavi dynasty

Atatürk's example was followed in Iran by Reza Khan (1878–1944), an army officer. He overthrew the last shah of the Kajar dynasty and declared himself shah of a new Pahlavi dynasty. His efforts to westernize Iran were much less successful, partly because he lacked Atatürk's popular support and partly because the hold of Islam on everyday life was stronger than in Turkey. His son, Mohammad Reza Shah Pahlavi (1919–1980), pushed westernization even harder. His push provoked a backlash that led to his overthrow and the establishment of an Islamic **republic** in 1979.

Nkrumah

Kwame Nkrumah (1909–1972) led the British West African **colony** of Gold Coast to independence in 1957 by largely peaceful means and became its first president. Nkrumah changed the country's name to Ghana, the name of a past great African empire. This new name was a clue to his long-term aim of bringing together former European colonies in Africa into a new united Africa, under the leadership of Ghana and himself. Nkrumah had spent many years abroad, studying in Britain and the United States. He promoted himself as a great thinker and published many books on political questions and the nature of African culture. Many think these books were written by other people.

Nkrumah (waving) chose to wear the robes of a chief to show respect for African tradition and independence from the West.

Ghana itself was, by African standards, well-off at independence, thanks to its thriving cocoa industry. Nkrumah used government revenue to build impressive buildings, create new industries, and support prestige projects like developing a national airline. In reality, these ventures were not what Ghana needed and they wasted resources that could have been better spent on improving such services as rural roads and basic healthcare. Nkrumah was in a hurry, though, to show results. He ignored the fact that most government-supported businesses were inefficient and corrupt. At the same time he devoted much of his time and energy to foreign travel and meetings because he was determined to show himself as a major international statesman. In the end, his efforts to create pan-African unity led nowhere.

Meanwhile, Nkrumah's methods of governing became increasingly dictatorial, as he blamed political opponents for his failure to turn Ghana into a major industrial power overnight. As early as 1958,

42

he introduced a law allowing suspected enemies to be arrested and imprisoned without trial and without any specific charge being made against them. The media was censored to publish only stories that made Nkrumah and Ghana look successful. Trade unions, universities, and the courts were brought under strict government control. In 1964, Nkrumah **decreed** that there would be only one political party and he would lead it. He stated that he would be president for the rest of his life.

In 1966, while Nkrumah was away in Beijing, the Ghanaian military seized power. Nkrumah's close friend, Sékou Touré, dictatorial president of Guinea, gave him a home. In 1972 Nkrumah died of cancer in Romania, where he had been offered treatment by the country's **communist** dictator, Nicolae Ceausescu. Nkrumah's magnificent presidential palace is now a forgotten ruin.

Castro

Cuba won its independence from Spain in 1902. The United States dominated its economy, however, and often interfered in its politics to protect American business interests. Fulgencio Batista was dictator of Cuba from 1952 to 1959. By this time, a few Cubans were very wealthy and most were very poor. Despite its large army, Batista's **regime** was overthrown by Cuban **exile** Fidel Castro (1927–) whose **guerrilla** force of a few dozen men turned into a tidal wave of discontent. Batista's soldiers and police simply crumbled before it.

Castro's regime confiscated much wealth, including many American-owned businesses, which led to a U.S. trade **embargo.** The embargo turned Castro to the U.S.S.R. as an alternative source of trade, aid, and weapons. Castro announced his conversion to communism and the **Soviet Union's** support became the mainstay of the economy.

Cuba's prosperity depended almost entirely on sugar, rum, and cigars, which were exported to the U.S.S.R. and its allies. In return, Cuba sent troops to fight for pro-Soviet movements in countries such as Angola.

Castro's **regime** stressed building up health and education for all. As a result Cubans have the highest life expectancy in Latin America (76 years) and a **literacy** rate of 96 percent, outranking neighboring Jamaica (86 percent) and resource-rich Brazil (84 percent). Sports were also given a high priority as a way of winning international prestige.

The Cuban Anier Garcia (center) takes the gold in the 110-meter hurdles at the 2000 Sydney Olympics. Cuban athletes, especially sprinters and boxers, have performed outstandingly internationally.

On the other hand, hundreds of thousands of Cubans hated Castro's rule so much that they risked death by drowning in dangerous and shark-infested seas. They left Cuba, usually headed to the United States, in small boats.

The collapse of the U.S.S.R. greatly damaged the Cuban economy, forcing it to build up tourism as an alternative source of income. Castro remains in power, but what will happen after his death is uncertain.

Plundering nations

Political scientists created the term "kleptocracy" (rule by thieves) to describe dictatorial governments that steal from a country for the personal benefit of the ruler and his close supporters. Many African countries are rich in resources but weak in institutions, and starved of skilled politicians to build them. They have provided dramatic examples of kleptocrats.

Bokassa

Jean-Bédel Bokassa (1921–1996) won numerous awards for bravery in the French colonial army before he became chief of staff of the newly independent Central African Republic. He seized power in a coup in 1966. Bokassa not only had opponents killed, but he personally took part in the murder of 100 schoolchildren.

After declaring himself president for life, Bokassa spent $20 million—a third of his government's annual revenue—on his **coronation.** "Emperor" Bokassa's coronation imitated that of his hero Napoleon.

45

For trade reasons, successive French governments supported Bokassa until an embarrassing scandal broke over a diamond given to French President Giscard d'Estaing. After Bokassa physically attacked the French ambassador, French paratroopers overthrew him by force, making it look like the coup was an internal affair. Bokassa fled to **exile.** He returned voluntarily in 1986 to serve seven years in prison for the murder of schoolchildren.

Amin

Idi Amin (1925–), though barely literate, became a senior officer of the Ugandan army under President Milton Obote (1924–), who relied on him to suppress opposition. Fearing Amin's power, Obote was about to replace him when Amin struck first. Amin initially gave the world's media the impression that he was a rather simple-minded, slightly ridiculous soldier. He soon resorted to rule by pure terror.

In 1972 the entire Asian business community was expelled so the new **regime** could plunder their property. The Asians were relatively fortunate. At least they got away with their lives, unlike the estimated 300,000 Ugandans who died under Amin's rule (1971–1979). Amin personally murdered dozens of people, including the Anglican archbishop. He fed many of his victims to crocodiles.

The economy fell into chaos. Despite the help of Libyan troops, Amin's forces collapsed to an invading army of Ugandan exiles who were supported by the army of neighboring Tanzania. Amin fled to safety in Libya and then Saudi Arabia, where he still lives.

Mobutu

Congo, fabulously rich with gold, diamonds, copper, cobalt, oil, and timber, was misruled from 1965 to 1997 by ex-soldier-turned-journalist President Mobutu (1930–1997). He was a former general who changed the country's name to Zaire as part of his plan to return the country to what he claimed was a genuinely African culture. For the same reason he changed his own name from Joseph-Désiré Mobutu to Mobutu Sese Seko Kuku Ngbendu Wa Za Banga ("the all-powerful warrior who, because of his endurance and inflexible will to win, will go from conquest to conquest, leaving fire in his wake").

Mobutu shared the vanity of Bokassa and Amin, but not their taste for murder. The damage he inflicted was caused more by corruption, neglect, and massive incompetence rather than by systematic cruelty. Protected by a bodyguard recruited from his own Ngbandi people, Mobutu used the rivalries of Congo's 250 other ethnic groups to provide excuses for the failures of his rule. By posing as a strong anti-**communist,** he also gained aid and military support from the United States, France, Belgium, and Israel. He also accepted military advisers from communist China and North Korea.

By the 1980s Mobutu's personal fortune was estimated at $4 billion. This estimate did not include his twenty overseas properties, valued at $37 million. Anti-communism ceased to protect Mobutu with the end of the Cold War in 1990, and during the 1990s he was on the defensive. In 1997 he was driven out by his own failing health and a rebel movement supported by democratic South Africa, the United States, and most of Zaire's neighbors. He died in exile.

Banda

The rule of ex-doctor Hastings Banda (1898–1997) in Malawi was far less bloody and chaotic than the three previous examples. Banda did, however, have political opponents jailed and executed. Scornful of the opinion of other black African leaders, Banda was happy to trade with South Africa. He accepted aid from the South African government, even though it oppressed its own black population. Living standards in Malawi rose slowly but steadily as Banda promoted himself from prime minister (1963) to president for life (1971). Banda's own living standards certainly rose, until senility forced him out. His death revealed that he had exported some $320 million to overseas bank accounts.

47

Ceausescu

The nearest the **communist** world has come to a kleptocracy is Romania under the rule of Nicolae Ceausescu (1918–1989). Ceausescu joined the illegal communist party as a teenager and was imprisoned for being a communist from 1936 to 1938 and again from 1940 to 1944. A member of the party's central committee at 27, it took twenty years for him to become general secretary. He then concentrated power in his own hands to become commander-in-chief and head of state as well.

Ceausescu appointed family members to positions of power which they used to enrich themselves. Meanwhile, to pay off Romania's foreign debts he forced the export of food and oil, causing acute shortages of both at home. In 1983, even TV was rationed to two hours a day, most of it about Ceausescu and his wife Elena, who were shown as brilliant leaders, adored everywhere they went. Ceausescu's plans to make Romania a powerful, modern country included ordering every family to have at least five children. Dozens of traditional villages were bulldozed to force people to live in apartment blocks, where they could be more easily controlled. Meanwhile, the Ceausescus and their family lived in luxurious palaces. Opposition was crushed by a 100,000-member police force, the Securitate.

On December 17, 1989, demonstrators protested in the provincial city of Timisoara. Hundreds were shot, provoking further protests in the capital, Bucharest, on December 21. The army sided with the protesters against the Securitate, and the rule of the Ceausescus ended with their flight, capture, and immediate trial for "crimes against the people," including the deaths of over 60,000. They were shot on December 25, 1989.

These five examples give a mixed record. Bokassa left a poor country poorer still. Amin, Mobutu, and Ceausescu reduced resource-rich countries to poverty and disorder. Banda provided stability and a measure of prosperity, but the millions of dollars he took could have been used to benefit his people.

⑦ How Dictatorships End

Searching for stability

Mexico—after the revolution of 1910–1920—and Atatürk's Turkey did grow into **democracies.** In twentieth-century Spain, Greece, Chile, Argentina, and Brazil, democracy has been successfully restored after periods of dictatorial or military rule. In Nigeria, Pakistan, Thailand, and Peru, the military has repeatedly intervened in politics, leading to periods of strongman rule by generals. However, their armed forces have also repeatedly shown a willingness to go back to their barracks and turn the problems of running the country back to **civilian** politicians.

Communist collapses

The breakup of the **Soviet Union** in 1990–1991 enabled the populations of its former allies in eastern Europe to overthrow their own communist governments through mass **demonstrations.** Poland was already well on the way to democracy thanks to its Solidarity movement, based on its trade-unions. In East Germany and Czechoslovakia, the change was almost bloodless; in Romania it was violent. The ending of the Cold War has made the United States less willing to maintain links with dictatorial governments simply because they claim to be anti-communist. This, and increasing public anger in western democracies at human rights abuses, has made it harder for dictatorships to benefit from trade and contacts with democratic countries and the global corporations based in them. One result has been the general disappearance of dictatorships in Latin America since the 1980s.

Death and disorder

As in the world of ancient Greece, the death of a dictator alone can be enough to end his **regime.** The end of a regime, however, can lead to chaos rather than freedom and stability.

Yugoslavia's wartime guerrilla leader Marshal Tito (1892–1980) managed to create a communist **state** that was fiercely independent of the U.S.S.R. He also controlled the tensions between the country's different nationalities. Tito left behind a leadership team that maintained this stability for a decade. Old rivalries between Serbs, Croats, and Bosnians eventually led to disastrous wars and the emergence of **authoritarian regimes** under Slobodan Milosevic in Serbia and Franjo Tudjman in Croatia. In neighboring Albania, the death of Enver Hoxha in 1985 ended 40 years of **communist** dictatorship. The end of the dictatorship left Albania the poorest country in Europe. A decline into general criminality followed. The crime levels continue to threaten the stability of its Balkan neighbors.

Family ties

Perhaps remarkably, family loyalties can still prove as important in some twentieth-century **states** as they were in medieval kingdoms, where sons followed fathers onto the throne.

In regimes dominated by a single leader, a funeral offers the opportunity to show loyalty. Here Bashar al-Assad, successor and son of Syrian ruler Hafez al-Assad, accompanies his father's coffin.

On the poor Caribbean island of Haiti, François "Papa Doc" Duvalier ruled from 1957 to 1971 using a mixture of corruption and terror. He gained support from the rural black poor against the traditionally powerful mulatto (mixed race) elite of the towns. He even managed to pass his position to his teenage son, Jean-Claude "Baby Doc" Duvalier, who was not overthrown until 1986. The United States has attempted to stabilize Haiti by using troops to guarantee order and by supervising elections to be sure they are fair. Despite these attempts, Haiti has remained prone to political violence.

North Korea is the only remaining state to cling to the hard-line communism of Stalin's day. The dictator Kim Il-Sung (known as the "Great Leader") ruled from 1948 to 1994 and managed to pass his position to his son Kim Jong-Il (known as the "Dear Leader"). He has ruled ever since, despite the fact that the country's massive spending on weapons has impoverished it and brought widespread famine.

The cult of personality

Concentrating power in the hands of a single individual has led to the emergence of a cult of personality in both **fascist** and communist regimes. Concentrating loyalty on a personality not only increased the power of dictators, but also distracted attention from gaps or contradictions in their political programs. As long as the leader wields power everything is, by definition, under control. At its most extreme, the cult of personality presents the leader as a universal genius, worthy not just of obedience but of adoration and the highest sacrifice. Members of the Hitler Youth were required to swear, "to devote all my energies and my strength to the savior of our country, Adolf Hitler. I am willing and ready to give up my life for him, so help me God." Although Stalin himself was largely responsible for the defeats suffered by the Soviet army at the hands of German invaders, Soviet **propaganda** hailed him as a military genius.

Perhaps the most extreme personality cult was built up around the North Korean communist leader, Kim Il Sung (1912–1994), and his son and successor Kim Jong-Il (1941–), who is referred to by the media as, "The peerless commander, heaven on earth and savior of the Korean people." In February 2002, Kim Jong-Il's 60th birthday was marked by an inscription in his honor carved onto a mountainside in letters over 100 feet (34 meters) high.

Isolation

Officially, Libya has a People's Government that claims to have abolished its institutions, such as its police force and courts of law, and replaced them with committees of ordinary citizens. Actually, the country is controlled by Colonel Muammar al-Qaddafi, who has ruled since he overthrew the **monarchy** in 1969. Like Nkrumah in Ghana, Qaddafi has presented himself as a great thinker. The book he wrote, *Green Book,* sets out his "Third Universal Theory." He claims his theory is the key to solving all political and economic problems. Like Nkrumah, Qaddafi has tried to put himself at the head of a unity movement, in his case pan-Arab. He has supported terrorists in neighboring countries such as Egypt, Sudan, and Chad, as well as in Northern Ireland, supplying weapons, money, training, and a safe refuge. Although Qaddafi has had opponents killed at home and abroad, he aims to present himself as a simple Muslim with no personal taste for power or wealth. United Nations (UN) **sanctions** on travel and trade with Libya have kept the country isolated. Qaddafi's government has been able to survive, though, thanks to Libya's oil, which makes the country relatively wealthy in relation to its small population.

There is no pretense at **democracy** in the Iraq of Saddam Hussein. Effective dictator of Iraq since 1979, he used the country's oil wealth to bring jobs, welfare, and electricity to the poor. He gave many people good reasons to be grateful for his rule. A long war (1980–1988) against neighboring Iran cost hundreds of thousands of lives and brought no gains, but failed to shake his position. Neither did his invasion of neighboring Kuwait. Iraqi forces were thrown out of Kuwait by a U.S.-led coalition in 1991 at the cost of another 100,000 lives. Despite UN sanctions isolating Iraq ever since, Saddam Hussein remains in power. Surrounded by family members and close supporters from his home town of Takrit, he takes elaborate precautions against assassination and has personally murdered his opponents.

Huge paintings of Saddam Hussein dominate public places in Iraq. Dictators typically use a lot of resources to maintain their popularity and the belief in their right to rule. They create **propaganda** that can be seen in rallies, posters, **demonstrations**, newspapers, films, and school textbooks.

In 1975 Pol Pot (1925–1998), a founder of the local **communist** party, seized power in Cambodia with the backing of a **guerrilla** army of peasants known as the Khmer Rouge. The country had been badly affected by the spillover effects of war in neighboring Vietnam, which had killed 150,000 Cambodians and made 2 million homeless. Pol Pot's answer was to cut all contacts with the outside world and make Cambodia self-supporting by forcing city dwellers to work on the land.

53

His Khmer Rouge government banned money, religion, foreign languages, newspapers, radio, television, and even bicycles. Two million people, a quarter of the entire population, were killed or died of starvation before Pol Pot was overthrown by a Vietnamese invasion in 1979. Pol Pot led Khmer Rouge **guerrilla** resistance to Cambodia's new Vietnamese-backed government for another seventeen years. He finally lost control of the Khmer Rouge and was arrested by them. He died of natural causes before he could be tried for his crimes.

Can dictatorships survive?

The system of dictatorship as a way of governing may be in decline, but it is by no means dead. Remarkably, presidents Assad in Syria and Kim in North Korea managed to pass their positions to their sons, like tyrants in the ancient Greek world. It remains to be seen how long they can hang on to power. Both Saddam Hussein in Iraq and Qaddafi in Libya may also attempt to prepare the way for a successor from within their own families. A vicious struggle for power is just as likely, whatever they attempt or intend to do. Terror as a tool of political power is under attack internationally. In the long run, the ever freer movement of people and ideas will combat its use within **states** as well as between them. Dictatorship, as the ancient Greeks came to understand, is basically an unstable form of government and cannot endure.

8 So, What Is Dictatorship?

Dictatorship was known to the ancient Greeks, but only became common as a form of government after Napoleon. Modern dictatorship is distinguished by its ruthless use of force and its ability to create active support for its efforts to change society. The existence of strong alternative institutions, such as a **monarchy,** army, or church, has tended to limit the changes a dictatorship can bring about. When a dictatorship succeeds in destroying such institutions, its potential for the abuse of power greatly increases.

The most extreme dictatorships have brought disaster on their countries. Adolf Hitler aimed to rid the world of **communism** but instead ensured that half of Europe, including half of Germany itself, would be ruled by communists for half a century. The 1959 census figures for the U.S.S.R. make it possible to calculate that, thanks to Stalin's persecutions in the 1930s, its population was 20 percent smaller than it would otherwise have been. In 1958, Mao Zedong called on China to make a Great Leap Forward and create modern industries overnight. The results were failed harvests and mass-starvation. In 1966, he launched a Cultural Revolution to restore his personal leadership of the party. Led by fanatical young Red Guards, mobs attacked authority figures such as party officials, factory managers, and teachers. About half a million people were killed and the country's education system and industry were set back years.

The rapid destruction of the cruel Taliban **regime** in Afghanistan in 2001 shows that a dictatorship's own weapons can be turned against it. In the same year, the former dictator of Serbia, Slobodan Milosevic, was brought before an international court of justice for crimes against the peoples of the Balkans. Clearly, there is an emerging belief in the world community that such abuses of power must be stopped.

Timeline

138–78 B.C.E.	Sulla, Roman dictator
c.102–44 B.C.E.	Julius Caesar, Roman dictator
1513	Niccolo Machiavelli of Florence publishes *The Prince*, a handbook for ruthless rulers
1653–1658	Oliver Cromwell rules Britain as Lord Protector
1804–1815	Napoleon rules France as emperor
1819–1825	Simon Bolivar liberates former Spanish colonies of South America
1852–1870	Napoleon III rules a Second Empire in France
1914–1918	World War I
1917	**Communist** revolution overthrows the **monarchy** in Russia
1922	Mussolini's March on Rome
1923	General Primo de Rivera seizes power in Spain General Mustafa Kemal declares Turkey a **republic**
1928	Stalin becomes unopposed ruler of the **Soviet Union**
1933	Hitler comes to power in Germany
1936–1939	Francisco Franco wins civil war in Spain to become *Caudillo*
1945	Fascist **regime** overthrown in Germany
1949	George Orwell publishes *Nineteen Eighty-four*
1959	Fidel Castro overthrows Fulgencio Batista in Cuba
1962	Military takeover in Burma (Myanmar)
1966	General Suharto overthrows Ahmed Sukarno in Indonesia Kwame Nkrumah overthrown by a military coup in Ghana
1969	Colonel Muammar Qaddafi overthrows the monarchy in Libya
1973	General Pinochet seizes power in Chile
1975	Spain restored to **democracy** by King Juan Carlos I
1977	General Zia ul-Haq overthrows **civilian** rule of Zulfikar Ali Bhutto in Pakistan Jean-Bedel Bokassa of the Central African Republic crowns himself Emperor

1979	Ayatollah Ruhollah Khomeini leads an Islamic Revolution in Iran
	Idi Amin flees from Uganda
	Saddam Hussein becomes undisputed dictator of Iraq
1985	Collapse of communist dictatorship in Albania with death of Enver Hoxha
1986	"Baby Doc" Duvalier overthrown in Haiti
1989–1991	Breakup of the Soviet Union
1991	Overthrow of Colonel Mengistu in Ethiopia
1999	General Pervez Musharraf takes power in Pakistan
2001	Slobodan Milosevic charged with war crimes and crimes against humanity at an international **tribunal** in The Hague
2002	Saddam Hussein's 65th birthday is celebrated throughout Iraq despite his poor record on human rights

Sources for Further Research

Books

Ayer, Eleanor H. *Adolf Hitler*. Farmington Hills, Mich.: Gale Group, 1996.

Downing, David. *Benito Mussolini*. Chicago: Heinemann Library, 2001.

Downing, David. *Joseph Stalin*. Chicago: Heinemann Library, 2001.

Shields, Charles J. *Saddam Hussein*. Broomall, Penn.: Chelsea House Publishers, 2002.

Tames, Richard. *Fascism*. New York: Raintree Steck-Vaughn, 2001.

Taylor, David. *Adolf Hitler*. Chicago: Heinemann Library, 2001.

Thorne, James. *Julius Caesar: Conquerer and Dictator*. New York: Rosen Publishing Group, 2002.

Websites

CIA World factbook: http://www.cia.gov/cia/publications/factbook/

PBS site on Slobodan Milosevic: http://www.pbs.org/weta/dictator/

Key Figures in the History of Dictatorship

Mao Zedong. (1893–1976). Born a farmer's son, Mao became active in student politics, founding the Chinese Communist Party in 1921. Mao adapted **communist** theory to suit the needs of Chinese peasants, setting up a peasant-led commune at Jiangxi from 1931 to 1934. When Chinese Nationalists attacked it, he led 100,000 followers on a 6,000-mile (9,700 kilometer) Long March (1934–1936) to the safety of Yenan. Two-thirds of the marchers died, but from there Mao led **guerrilla** resistance to Japanese invasion and later defeated the Nationalists, declaring China an independent communist **state** in 1949. Mao ordered the disastrous Great Leap Forward (1958–1960) and the hugely destructive Cultural Revolution (1966–1969). He was an accomplished poet, and his political writings were regarded as works of genius by the fanatical young Red Guards who did his bidding. Despite his responsibility for up to 20 million deaths, Mao is still honored for ending years of foreign interference in China.

Péron, Juan. (1895–1974). Handsome, charming, a champion skier and fencer, Péron was a professional army officer who had lived in and admired Mussolini's Italy. As one of the military members who seized power in Argentina in 1943, Péron built up a personal following among trade unions there, which enabled him to become president in 1946. He was a brilliant public speaker but gained even more popularity through his glamorous wife, Evita (1919–1952), a minor actress with a genius for publicizing her charity work. Péron's attacks on foreign-owned businesses were as popular as his welfare reforms and support for local industry. Péron and Evita were truly adored by the poor and her sudden early death from cancer plunged the nation into grief. Péron then lost touch with the people, angered the powerful Catholic church and army, brought the economy to ruin, and was driven into **exile.** Support for Péronism survived, however, and in 1973 Péron returned to the country in triumph. However, he failed to solve Argentina's continuing problems and died after a year. His third wife, Isabelita (1931–), took over but was overthrown by the army in 1976.

Pinochet, Augusto. (1915–). A professional army officer, Pinochet led the Chilean military to overthrow the legally elected government of Salvador Allende, whose reforms for the poor were thought to damage business. Pinochet's government imprisoned, tortured, and murdered opponents and made life hard for the poor. However, he brought Chile prosperity. Pinochet himself passed power back to an elected president, but he kept his rank as army commander-in-chief, with immunity from the law for actions committed during his rule.

Sukarno, Ahmed. (1902–1970). A member of the anti-Dutch movement for Indonesian independence from its earliest days in the 1920s, Sukarno had an outstanding gift for languages and could move a mob to tears or frenzy in any of a dozen tongues. His great gift to his country was the creation of the modern Indonesian language, which united a nation of island-dwellers scattered over 3,000 miles (5,000 kilometers). As first president of an independent Indonesia, Sukarno's vanity led him to parade as a world statesman and waste Indonesia's natural wealth on grand projects that did nothing for the poor. Accused of corruption, he was overthrown by General Suharto (1921–), whose long period of military rule was even more corrupt, on an even greater scale. Suharto was driven into **exile** by a popular uprising in 1998.

Milosevic, Slobodan. (1941–). After a successful career as a **Communist** official, in 1988 Milosevic became president of Serbia, the most powerful part of Yugoslavia. His pro-Serb actions made him popular in Serbia but led Slovenia and Croatia to fight successfully for their independence. Milosevic encouraged Serb fighters in Bosnia to add lands under their control to Serbia. He then used Serb forces against the Albanian inhabitants of Kosovo, causing thousands more deaths and a massive refugee crisis. Within Serbia he and his family abused their position to enrich themselves and used bribery, violence, and rigged elections to stay in power. After his overthrow by opposition Serbs, Milosevic was handed over to an international **tribunal** at The Hague in 2001 and faced charges of war crimes and crimes against humanity.

Glossary

arbitrary acting on personal wishes, regardless of law or reason

aristocracy rule by those believed to be best qualified, often the wealthiest

authoritarian system of government that demands strict obedience, but does not try to control everything

caudillismo tradition of rule by a single dictator in Spanish-speaking countries

chancellor high political official

charismatic having extraordinary powers of personality

city-state city, and sometimes its surrounding area, that is independent

civilian person who is not a member of the army or police force

colony territory ruled by another country

communism belief in a government based on the idea that a single ruling political party can run a country for the benefit of all of its peoples better than if they are left to make their own decisions and keep their own private homes, land, and businesses

constitution set of rules setting out how a system of government should work

coronation religious ceremony making a ruler the rightful monarch by giving him or her a crown

decree statement having the force of law

democracy system of government by the whole population. Voters usually elect representatives who govern the country.

demonstration parade or mass meeting in support of a cause

despot absolute ruler or tyrant

embargo order by a government that limits trade, often forbidding all imports and exports, with a certain country

exile living in another country for political reasons

fascism system of dictatorship that puts the nation before the individual and forbids opposition

guerrilla member of a small armed group fighting against a larger, regular army

ideology organized system of ideas to be put into practice through political action

industrialization bringing jobs that involve mass production of goods

junta Spanish word for a group of military officers who have seized power by force

leisure time off for recreation

literacy ability to read or write

massacre systematic killing of large numbers of people

military dictator dictator whose power depends on control of soldiers rather than a political party

militia part-time armed force of volunteers

monarchy system of government in which a country is ruled by a king or queen

Nazi short name of the National Socialist German Workers' Party (Nationalsozialistiche Deutsche Arbeiterpartei), led by Adolf Hitler. The Nazis ruled Germany from 1933 to 1945. Nazism was the German form of fascism.

pagan believer in pre-Christian gods

parliament group of people that writes laws for a country

partisan armed volunteer fighter who is not part of a regular, professional army

patriot person who loves his or her country

post-colonial independent state that was once a colony

propaganda communication through messages and symbols aiming to persuade people to support a particular point of view, usually through appealing to emotion rather than reason

regime system or style of government

reprisal action taken to punish another action

republic country in which power is held by people, or by their elected representatives, and not by a monarch. A republic often has an elected president as head of state.

rule of law situation in which citizens are treated fairly, according to known rules applied equally to all

SA (Sturmabteilung) storm troopers: the Nazi Party militia

SS (Schutzstaffel) defense squadron: Hitler's personal bodyguards. The SS eventually grew into a Nazi party army with hundreds of thousands of members.

sanction limit on trade or other contacts to punish a country

secret police police, usually in civilian clothes, who operate in secret and outside the control of the law and court system, often using threats, torture, and murder

secular non-religious

Slav person speaking one of the Slavic languages such as Russian, Polish, or Bulgarian

socialist person who believes in using government to make the lives of citizens more equal

Soviet Union the Union of Soviet Socialist Republics (U.S.S.R.), a communist empire governed by Russia that lasted from 1922 to 1991

state independent country

suppressed held back or preventing from happening

technocrat person with special skills of management, especially good at running large organizations

totalitarian type of dictatorship that aims at complete control over every aspect of people's lives

tribunal court of justice

tyranny rule by an oppressive or cruel ruler, called a tyrant

Index